ALSO BY FREDERICK FRANCK:

Days with Albert Schweitzer   1959

My Friend in Africa   1960

African Sketchbook   1961

My Eye Is in Love   1963

Outsider in the Vatican   1965

I Love Life   1967

Exploding Church   1968

Simenon's Paris   1969

The Zen of Seeing   1973

An Encounter with Oomoto   1975

READERS:

Au Pays du Soleil   1958

Au Fil de l'Eau   1964

Croquis Parisiens   1969

Tutte le Strade Portano a Roma   1970

The Book of Angelus Silesius

 Vintage Books : A Division of Random House, New York

The Book of
Angelus Silesius

With observations
by the ancient Zen Masters

Johann Scheffler

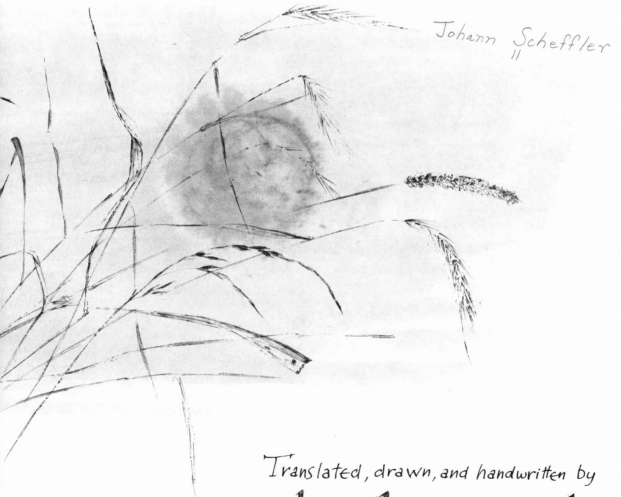

Translated, drawn, and handwritten by

Frederick Franck

Vintage Books   A Division of Random House, New York

Published in the United States by Random House Inc., New York, and simultaneously in Canada by Random House of Canada Ltd., Toronto. Distributed by Random House, Inc. New York. Originally published by Alfred A. Knopf, Inc., 1976

The observations by the Eastern Masters are taken mostly from the treasure house of Mahayana Buddhism, which during twenty-five years has provided my daily reading, in translations by Wong Mou-lam, D.T. Suzuki, R.H. Blyth, Charles Luk, John Blofeld, Garma C.C. Chang, and others. Except where attributed, they are quoted from memory, and in the form in which they have become my own.

If one should wonder why I have drawn so heavily on a limited number of these Masters — such as Hui Neng, Ikkyu, Sengtsan — the explanation is simple: it is these teachers who have meant most to me in everyday life, as proven friends.

The poems by Ikkyu, Basho, Ryoto, in the translation by the late R.H. Blyth, as well as his translation of Sengtsan's Hsinhsinming, are used by the gracious permission of Hokuseido Press, Tokyo.

f.f.

LIBRARY OF CONGRESS CATALOGING IN PUBLICATION DATA
Scheffler, Johannes, 1624-1677
The book of Angelus Silesius (i.e. Johannes Scheffler),
the 17th-century European Zen poet whose verses form a bridge
between the mysticism of the East and West.

Translation of selections from "Cherubinischer Wandersmann."
I. Franck, Frederick (1909-   ) II. Title: The book of
Angelus Silesius (i.e. Johannes Scheffler), the 17th-century
European Zen poet.
PT1791.S2C513   1976   831'.5   75-39074
ISBN 0-394-71641-8

For my friends and companions on the Way,
whether I have ever met you or not...
For all who in the noise of our time
feel the need of a new inwardness... For all
who may share my delight in discovering
a Western Zen-poet...

... great truths do not interest the multitudes,
and now that the world
is in such confusion,
even though I know the Path,
how can I guide?
I know I cannot succeed
and that trying to force results
I shall merely add to the confusion.
Isn't it better to give up and
stop striving?

But then, if I do not strive,
who will?

                   —Chuang-Tzu

Do not show your poem to a non—poet...
                   — Mumonkan

contents

The Book of
Angelus Silesius

introduction

Since this is a person-to-person book, I write it to you in longhand. Of course, this will slow up writing as well as reading, but then, this is not a book for speedreading! Each verse and every quotation from the Eastern Masters deserves being pondered in the heart. A few minutes of "pointed mindfulness" add more to our life-experience than several years of rushing while sleepwalking. For meditation takes place "across the line called time," in the timeless.

If I did not think this to be a necessary book, I would not have written it. Necessary for whom?

For my friends and companions on the Way, whether I have met them or not. For all those who in the noise of our time feel a new need for inwardness. For all who may share my delight in discovering a Western Zen poet, who expresses in the traditional language of our own culture what we are apt to believe only the enlightened ones of the East have attained. For in this Western Zen poet I found a bridge between the essential insights of East and West. Such a bridge is proof —ever needed again— that although human beings from the East and the West may differ in many things, they share the Inner Light, the Buddha Nature—to paraphrase Hui Neng. If I had another hundred years to live, I would postpone finishing this book. But alas, I don't have another century, at most a few years, one, or two, or ten.

This book is essentially a translation of a little book I re-discovered while browsing in a secondhand bookshop in Copenhagen on a stopover during my third trip to Japan. Its title: _Der Cherubinische Wandersmann_ ("The Cherubinic Wanderer"). Its author: the 17th-century mystical poet Angelus Silesius, who lived in a century of upheavals, wars, and revolutions, a time of religious conflict, almost as troubled as ours.

I had first read it as a medical student in Holland, where I was born. It had made an impression on me then, this collection of deceptively naïve, mystical rhymes, which I remembered

finding much too pious at the time. Some I still recalled
vaguely.

That night in my Copenhagen hotel room they opened up in
their full and rather awesome profundity, these little rhymes
written by a man who died three hundred years ago. He had
written them during four days and nights of illumination,
satori — in direct confrontation with That which he addressed
as God.

The eyes which reread Angelus Silesius, however, had been
opened meanwhile by some twenty-five years of almost daily
Zen study, and as I was reading, it was as if the ancient
Zen Masters, who had become my companions and friends,
were bending over me, whispering their own—sometimes quite
ironic—commentaries in my ear.

It was a fascinating spiritual entertainment and I decided
then and there to translate Angelus Silesius into English and
let the Oriental echoes be the running commentary, leaving it
to the reader in his meditation and free association to judge
their relevancy, their contradictions and agreements.

෴

It is only fair to post a few warnings. First of all: I am
no Scholar. I am an artist. All I really know in my bones
I have experienced in a discipline I call SEEING/DRAWING. *)
It is my way of meditation, my yoga, my zazen. SEEING/DRAWING
is the discipline (or yoga) which brings me into intimate, living
contact with the world around me, and through it with myself.
HuiNeng (637-715 A.D.) says: "The Truth is not seen into by sitting
in Silent meditation." Another Master, Daie, assures us that "Zen
practiced in a State of activity is far Superior to that practiced
in quietude."

My meditations in preparation for this book are the simple
drawings of leaves and plants in a Small garden of Biblical
flora I found as an oasis in a run-down neighborhood of New
York, behind the Cathedral of St. John the Divine.
Not that I am much of a Cathedral-man! I am not strong at
praying. Yet, before I start drawing, it often happens that
suddenly the utter poignancy of a cloud Sailing through
the Sky, of a bent old back, or a child with its balloon-treasure
moves me — and that I hear myself say, "Oh God!", I, who

*) "The Zen of Seeing — Seeing/drawing as meditation" N.Y. 1973.

when asked, "Do you believe in God" am most apt to shrug:
"I believe in nothing but God !"
I also still catch myself, at moments of unbearable joy, awe
or sadness, making a little sign of the cross over my heart.
It is an old, inexplicable gesture from childhood: I did not grow up
as a Catholic. I cannot help it, and it is perhaps the only true prayer
I have ever known.

Angelus Silesius was born Johannes Scheffler in 1624, the son of
Stanislaus Scheffler, a well-to-do Lutheran who had emigrated from
Poland, where Protestants were under strong Catholic pressure.
Breslau, capital of Silesia, was solidly Lutheran. Stanislaus, at age
sixty-two, started his new life there by marrying the daughter of
a court physician, a girl who was forty years younger than he.
They had three children, of whom Johannes was the first. The father
died at age seventy-five and his young wife followed him two years
later, when Johannes was fourteen. It is not known who looked after
the Scheffler orphans and sent Johannes for his secondary education
to the highly regarded Elizabeth Gymnasium, where he discovered
his taste for poetry. He graduated in 1643 and traveled, across a
Germany torn by the Thirty Years War, to the University of
Strasbourg, where he enrolled as a medical student. After a

few years he transferred to Leyden in Holland, one of the oldest
and most famous universities, and finished his medical training
at the University of Padua in 1648.

Seventeenth-century Holland was an island of tolerance in the
ocean of religious prejudice and persecution of post-Reformation
Europe. Here Spanish Jews fleeing the Inquisition as well as the
most outlandish Protestant sects found freedom of speech. At
Leyden young Scheffler became involved with an interdenominational
circle of mystics and met the much older Silesian nobleman Von
Franckenberg, who had brought the manuscripts of "the inspired
shoemaker," Jakob Boehme, from Görlitz to Holland, where they
could be printed. Franckenberg became Scheffler's intimate friend
and mentor. From tolerant, yet Calvinistic and Puritan Holland,
Scheffler plunged into the sensuous Italian atmosphere of the
University of Padua, with its emotional Catholic devotions,
processions, and colorful ceremonial. He received his M.D. from
Padua, and as a twenty-three-year-old doctor he returned
to Silesia and through family connections was almost immediately
appointed as court physician to the Duke of Öls.

On a nearby estate his friend Franckenberg lived in
seclusion, meditation and study. The fanatical Lutheran clergy
suspected Franckenberg — who never appeared for confession
and communion — of heresy, and attacked him openly from the

pulpit. It was Franckenberg who initiated young Scheffler into the writings of the great European mystics, especially the world of the great theosophist Boehme. Scheffler soon published a collection of religious hymns. They were promptly condemned as being in conflict with Lutheran theology in their praise of "good works," their all too "Catholic" attitudes toward Christ, but even more because of their "pantheistic views" on God's presence even in animals and plants.

Franckenberg died suddenly in 1652 and left Scheffler a lonely man, utterly isolated in the provincial town of Öls, which was almost solidly and narrowly Lutheran. He found some understanding only among Catholics, especially the local Jesuits. The Society of Jesus had been mobilized, and Jesuits were sent into Silesia in ever-increasing numbers to achieve by peaceful means what the Thirty Years War had failed to do in this region: stamp out Protestantism. In Moravia and Bohemia, Hussites and Lutherans had been exterminated by the Hapsburg Emperors. After peace was signed at last, the task of reconquering Silesia for Mother Church was entrusted to Jesuit missionaries, who went to work with zeal and intelligence, and who were glad to welcome the prominent physician-poet with his mystical gifts and his Saint Francis-like tenderness for the animal world.

Scheffler's friendship with the hated Jesuits made him an object of persecution, and soon after Franckenberg's death he lost his position at court. A few months later, in 1653, he became a Catholic. He felt himself to be reborn and assumed a new name, Angelus Silesius: "God's Silesian Messenger." Meanwhile, having become a favorite target for bitter and hateful denunciations on the part of the Lutheran clergy, he involved himself in the constant disputes and controversies that were to erode his extraordinary spiritual gifts. After "The Cherubinic Wanderer," he continued to write but never recovered the heights of inspiration which made the "Wanderer" a masterpiece that earned him his place in the history of mystical literature. It consists of the 302 verses written during his four days of illumination. No details are known of this prolonged enlightenment experience other than those revealed in the volume itself in full intensity and authenticity: these verses may well contain the most direct, articulate and accessible record of such a crucial experience ever bequeathed us by a Western mystic.

That it was valid for Christians across denominational borders was proven when, less than half a century after Johannes' death, "The Cherubinic Wanderer" was reprinted with an introduction by the prominent historian of religion Gottfried Arnold, which reclaimed the poet's work for Protestantism; and so "The Cherubinic Wanderer" became integrated in the shared heritage of Protestant and Catholic Europe. Strangely it never became widely known in America.

I do not pretend to be a connoisseur of poetry, certainly not of seventeenth-century German poetry. But whether "The Cherubinic Wanderer" is superb poetry or merely naive rhyme, it provides a rare opportunity to meet a mystic who is exceptionally articulate in expressing the depths of his experience, and this with such simplicity, force and directness that — for me — the split between Christian God-language and the God-free language of the Buddhist contemplatives becomes relatively unimportant and can be forgotten.

Many of our contemporaries have become severely allergic to God-language. It is somehow suspect of guilt by association. For too long it has been mouthed mechanically and all too often for purposes of forceful indoctrination and manipulation.

But when mystics like Angelus Silesius speak of God, they do

So from a level and an intensity of awareness, and in a tone of voice one trusts at once.

Angelus Silesius parrots no one. He has experienced what he speaks of. His God, although addressed as a Person, is what others have spoken of as the Groundless Ground, or Ultimate Reality, or the Immutable Law that governs all beings and is to be found reflected in the depths of the human heart.

As one of the many who have made their spiritual detour via the East in their quest for Meaning, and who have become familiar with both the Eastern and Western terms men have used to express their experience of the Real, I had little trouble shuttling back and forth between the language of the Western mystic and that of the Eastern contemplatives. Here and there I found a verse that resisted this easy shuttling, that seemed merely moralistic, or pious. These verses I omitted from the translation.

Johannes Scheffler must have jotted down his Illuminations as they came. In an effort to make the work more accessible, I ordered the verses I selected according to ten main themes. My selection, a very personal one, comprises more than half of the original verses. I have made no

12

attempt to force them into Alexandrines. My concern was to be faithful to the poet's spirit as I understood it. I had to take many liberties in trying to find equivalents in more or less modern English, while retaining some of the seventeenth-century patina. I use the term "the Me" where Angelus Silesius refers to the isolated, separate ego, that "empirical ego" which we imagine ourselves to be and attempt to impose on others.

Angelus Silesius is a Christian, although an unconventional one—and in every breath he mentions God, love, sin, prayer, heavenly bliss. To the Zen man these words mean little or nothing. But when the poet talks about human fate and foibles and of his firsthand experience of what lies beyond, when he speaks about ego and what lies beyond ego he is a radical for whom God is the unknown Mystery, Nothingness, Abyss. Here the Zen Master would understand him perfectly. Are they perhaps speaking in different words of a very similar experience?

The Silesian mystic stood in God's presence during his four days of ecstasy. The Zen Masters simply stood in the Presence, in the Present, in the Now/Here. Both must speak of their most momentous experience, as if to tell us: TRUST YOUR DEEPEST INTUITIONS! YOU ARE NOT ALONE! YOU ARE NOT MAD!

YOU ARE NOT LOSING YOUR WAY! YOU ARE ON YOUR WAY!
YOU ARE YOUR WAY!

Both disdain abstract language and metaphysical niceties. They
speak of what they have experienced, and they do this with
directness and in few words. They both love paradoxes that
shock the mind out of its safe, logical rut, paradoxes that, for a
change, force logic to be the servant rather than the master of
experience, that prod the mind to overcome all contradictions
and dualities.

Both speak person-to-person, not to an audience. There never is an
audience, they know, only a human heart somewhere that responds.
The human heart has no plural.

Of course they must speak the language of their time and culture.
Angelus Silesius could not help being conditioned by the language of the
Gospels, and of the mystics who came before: Eckhart, Tauler, Ruysbroeck,
Boehme. The Zen poets and sages are steeped in the language of
the Sutras, of Hui Neng, Rinzai, Huang Po.

Both are driven to communicate, to transmit — however imperfectly —
what they have seen. Here imperfection becomes perfection:
to express the Inexpressible for the benefit of others is the highest
human challenge. But here it must be realized that for the

awakened Spirit there is no longer a split between "I" and "other."
The awakened Spirit has only one desire left : to share the Bread
of Life it has found with those that are still seeking and hungry,
but are no longer "other".

"I am neither I nor other" seems to be the revelation shared
by all who have transcended the bonds of ego, in East as well
as West.

In my own search for That Which Matters, I found in Zen, so
many years ago, a full confirmation of my intuition that I,
like every other human being, contain a hidden but incorruptible
core. It is hidden underneath immense layers of confusion,
neurosis and delusion. Yet it is our true center. It is our truly
HUMAN nature. It is our very core of sanity! The sayings of
the Zen Masters speak of this core in a variety of terms: Bodhi,
Suchness, Self-Nature, Buddha-Nature, the Original Face, the
Essence of Mind, the True Self, the Unborn, the True-Man-
without-Label-in-this-mass-of-red-flesh.
When they speak of Enlightenment, Satori, Awakening, Liberation,
they refer to the breakthrough, the full awareness, the realization
of this hidden core, this mysterious ingredient that I share with
all beings, but that is unattainable by intellectual effort. It is

unattainable by what Buddhists call "the ego-mind." It is, the Zen Masters insist, "neither dependent on nor independent of this ego."

Might this True Self, etc., not be what in Christian language is spoken of as "The Light That Lighteth Every Man That Cometh into the World," the "Inner Light," "The Kingdom Within," "The Birth of God in the Soul," "The Indwelling Spirit"?

Could Christ be the Master who summons man to find the True Self, and his Sermon on the Mount the self-revelation of the Enlightened man and the values he lives by?

We are born illiterate... But it is more important to realize that we are born in complete ignorance of who we are, and what it is to be human. If our lives are to be lived as human lives, we have to discover our fundamental and specific humanness: the True-Man-without-Label-in-this-mass-of-red flesh.

Discovering the True Man requires first of all that we discover and relinquish bit by bit what we are NOT, peeling off layer after layer of the onion, all the layers formed by our conditioning, our training, our culture.

Then what remains? That Which Matters remains! And if we fail to discover That, because of fear, confusion, weakness or inertia, we die as not quite full grown, not quite human animals. If we do discover It, we die too, but at any rate we have not lived the extraordinary human adventure in vain. The question is: How to discover it? Is it true, as one is often told: "You can't learn it from a book"?

It depends on WHICH book and how you read it. I have learned more from the right book (and the more right it was, the more often I had to read it) than from the wrong guru... To find the right guru, teacher or spiritual guide is about as difficult as to find the right mate or even the right psycho-therapist.

"The wisdom of the past, present, and future Buddhas, as well as of all the Scriptures is in our mind. But in case we fail to enlighten ourselves we have to seek the guidance of the learned and pious ones. On the other hand, those who enlighten themselves need no outside help. It is wrong to insist that without the advice of the learned and pious we cannot attain liberation, because it is by our innate wisdom that we enlighten ourselves," says Hui Neng.

The real master is the one who knows that no one can teach another, and that it is his own quality of _being_ itself

that is the catalyst in the other's process of discovery.
The Sutra of Hui Neng, the works of D.T.Suzuki, the
first chapter of St.John's Gospel have been to me such
teachers, such friends on the Way. And so have the great painters
whose actual subject was Suchness: the ancient Chinese, and Vermeer
and Rembrandt... and in music Bach and Purcell and Mozart.
They are the great friends, always ready to restore our faith in
the Human. They open our eyes and ears by allowing the True
Man in them to speak openly, fearlessly, shamelessly across
space, time, and death.
Angelus Silesius, in the quaint language of his rhymes, has joined them.
The Real needs neither exoticism nor picturesque disguise. It
is only secret, hidden by its simplicity.
Hui Neng also says: "THE MEANING OF LIFE IS TO SEE."
Seeing/Drawing a tree, a leaf, a human face reveals this
hidden simplicity.

It would be foolhardy to present a Western and Christian
mystic as a Zen poet if Zen were to be understood as "a religion."
It is not. Nor is it necessarily tied to Buddhism. Zen is rather
an attitude of openness toward life itself, a quality of
awareness, an intuitive grasping hold of the "structure of Reality"

as I have come to call it – that underlies all religions, that is root and quintessence of all religious experience.

Everyone knows by now that Zen resists all definition. There is no Zen except the Zen that is experienced. One can, however, give some hints about its nature. The broadest of these hints was given by Bodhidharma, who according to legend brought Zen from India to China in the fifth century:

A special transmission outside the scriptures
not depending on words and letters
but directly pointing at the Mind (or "Heart")
of man, making him see into
the Nature itself and thus attaining awakening,
Buddhahood.

All attempts to describe Zen in Western philosophical, psychological, or metaphysical terms are completely misleading, for Zen is neither philosophy nor ideology: it is an experience in which that which philosophy philosophizes about is grasped concretely. The Zen experience is unattainable by the isolated, separate, illusory ego, whatever "expansion of consciousness" it may achieve as an isolated ego.

"ALL BEINGS ARE THE BUDDHA-NATURE," says Dogen (thirteenth century). A Christian version of this awesome saying might be: "Every heart is the vessel from which Christ waits to be born."

But Zen would counter: "There is not anything new to be born. It has been within you from the beginningless beginning. It has only to be awakened, to become aware of itself in you."

The Zen experience is the breakthrough into our consciousness of the Indwelling Spirit, the Buddha-Nature. Suddenly, freed from the imaginings and illusions of the ego, we see our actual, our real relationship to ourselves, to all other beings and to the Whole. It is a relationship of infinite interdependence. Henceforth all acts that harm a fellow being become inconceivable, not because of some external ethics, but because of the insight gained.

Since it is simpler to state what Zen is NOT than to say what it is, let me first say what it definitely isn't!

Zen is not: mysticism, quietism, or withdrawal from the world.

Zen is not: "calming the mind" (or "emptying the mind"), sitting in thoughtless meditation.

Zen is not :   asceticism, nor is it pantheism. It is not an ism
             at all.

Zen is not :   a value system. It is no "system." It is, however,
             close to being Value as such.

Zen is not :   an addition to Reality, nor does it subtract a
             jot from it or distort it. Zen cannot be
             decadent for it is always concretely in touch
             with the inner workings of life itself: it is
             intensely realistic.

Zen does not: see our relative everyday reality as
             opposed to Ultimate Reality. For Zen the
             relative IS absolute, the Absolute IS relative.

When a Master was asked: "What is the Tao?" he answered:
"It is right before your eyes."
"So why can't I see it?"
"Because you have a Me."

Zen is : escape from the Me to the True Self. From illusion
         to Reality, from the madhouse into sanity.

Zen is : Life that knows it is living – love of life

21

experienced _ life expressed inwardly and directly, without
adornment _ in art, religion, love, humor.

Zen is : Seeing the world, my cat, my wife, myself not JUST as
they are, but SUCH as they are.

Zen is : that which joins what our rationalizations have torn
asunder, and tears apart what they have joined.

Zen is : time experienced as timelessness, eternity. And eternity
as time, as Now / Here.

Zen is : Where the commonplace is no longer banal but wondrous,
where the natural is perceived as supernatural:
"How miraculous, I draw water, I carry fire wood! I
blink my eyes! This skeleton dances, talks, makes love!..."

Zen is : the living life in me, aware of itself as the life that is
shared by all beings.

Zen is : discovered _ after long preparation _ when it reveals itself
in a flash of insight.

If Zen is intensely realistic, it is no less intensely spiritual.
For Zen there is no split, no duality, between the material
world and the spiritual world. It is the same world, only seen
from a different viewpoint. Neither is there an Absolute
Reality that stands over and against our "relative," everyday

reality. Both are the very same reality – if seen by the awakened eye. Zen here disagrees with Hindu thought, for which all phenomena, all beings are sheer Maya, illusion. Zen does not see beings and things as illusion: The illusion is to see them as separate, isolated existences. Our habit of looking upon ourselves and other beings and objects as having autonomy, independence, permanence, is from the viewpoint of Zen our all-pervading hallucination.

"When is a man in mere understanding?" asks Meister Eckhart. "When he sees one thing as separated from another."
"And when is a man above mere understanding?"
"When a man sees All in all, then a man stands beyond mere understanding."

On the flyleaf of a book I found something dated August, 1955, scribbled in the lobby of a luxury hotel in Europe as I was kept waiting for some personage who, at that moment, seemed important enough to wait for.
"I walk naked in my clothes, within my skin.

That which looks through these eyes and watches
is from eternity to eternity
watching itself motionlessly going through the motions."

I remember thus meeting myself when and where least expected.
I am still walking "thus" and hope this book may be your
companion as you walk thus — naked and within your skin.

What working on this book has done for me, and what I hope it
may do for you, is to bridge the chasm between East and West.
The two have never been separated by any chasm except one
of our own making.
In each of us lives this "East" as well as this "West," just as
in each of us lives both a man and a woman. Men who
repress their female side, woman who deny their masculine
traits, mutilate themselves, stunt their growth to full
humanity.
BY DENYING OUR "EAST," WE HAVE BECOME LIKE
MACHINES WITH OVERDEVELOPED COMPUTER BRAINS.
Denying their "West," some Eastern societies may have
stagnated.
No one can deny or starve half of his humanity with

impunity. Western man has become a hustling sleepwalker, unlikely to wake up on his seventy-year sleepwalking tour, racing like a rat toward all the knowledge the darkened ego-mind can gather, all the know-how that produced the gas ovens of the Nazis and was blown to bits at Hiroshima.

At last we feel we must turn inward and are driven to recover our full humanity and its meaning. It is revealing that, turning East, we find Upanishads and Sutras more compatible and accessible than the writings of the mystics of our own culture. The detour via the East has become indispensable in our search for home.

Yet, the mystics of the East and of the West have never been separated by a chasm. Both have trusted the indelible imprint in the heart of each human being that enables it to become fully human, however great the differences in language or symbol system they use to express it.

To pretend that all religions are "the same" is as superficial as it is untrue. One might as well say that Madras curry and strawberry sundae are the same, since both are food. Religions were born in very different cultural climates. Each speaks in its own language of man's irrepressible concern with Ultimate Meaning, and each one points to the overcoming of ego as the precondition for the perception of this Meaning. To make a hodgepodge of their vocabularies and concepts is confusing rather than helpful. On the other hand, to notice parallels and convergences has become unavoidable, for we are becoming less and less imprisoned within set cultural borders.

The world is fast becoming a single spiritual continent. Symbols and concepts (yes, even God versus no-God) may clash in the brain, yet fuse quite naturally in the much more clairvoyant heart. Our spiritual home is where the heart is.

Hui Hai in the ninth century spoke the definitive word on this underlying unity. He was asked: "Do Confucianism, Taoism, and Buddhism really amount to three teachings or to one?" He answered: "As understood by men of great understanding they are the same. For men of mediocre understanding they differ. All of them spring from the functioning of the same Self-Nature. It is views involving differentiation that make them three. Whether a man gains Illumination or remains deluded depends on himself, not on differences and similarities in doctrine."

And when a Master, while testing a pupil, scoffed at his origin, the

26

pupil replied: "Men from the North and men from the South may differ, but both have the Buddha-Nature."

Just as there never was a group of painters who called themselves "Impressionists" (the word was coined by a critic as an epithet) there was never a "mystic" who considered himself anything but a realist. He had seen Reality with his own eyes, had been in living contact with it. Suddenly the merciless "realism" of politicians, the know-how without wisdom of practical men, seemed wildly unrealistic, a dangerous conceit. He had seen how it constantly made for a false appraisal of situations, and hence habitually missed its targets, causing frustration, suffering, and catastrophe. Against this disastrously naïve realism the mystic proclaimed the mature realism of the awakened heart which is both Wisdom and Compassion.

The mystics of history who are still remembered are the ones who tried to communicate their vision of Reality to others. They would have kept silent if they had despaired of the potentiality of their fellowmen of breaking through "common sense." They trusted the latent capacity lying dormant in human beings, only waiting to be roused from its suspended animation.

Only recently has modern psychology, after a century or more of concentration on mental abnormalities, started to study healthy, integrated human beings.

And soon it discovered in the history of these quite normal people what became known as "peak experiences" that had never been forgotten, moments in which these ordinary mortals had felt Reality break through, and when, in a flash, life in its inexpressible fullness had opened up and they were overwhelmed with an ineffable, unforgettable bliss.

This is the kind of revelation that had always been regarded as the monopoly of privileged mystics. It was found to be within the reach of normal human experience. It may well be _the_ human experience par excellence....

I remember with absolute clarity, as I am sure you must remember, such flashes of utter wonder and exultation, of the direct perception of being alive. It may have happened while looking into the yellow heart of a daisy and seeing it look back at you, or when seeing a familiar face suddenly reveal itself as if for the first time or when you heard the rain beating against a windowpane, or when suddenly sun burst on a meadow through black clouds. Such experiences one remembers as long as one lives. They are the root experiences of art and of religion; they are the first manifestations of the True Man within.

All too often these first intimations of wonder at the visible world ("The mystical is not the how of the world, but that it exists," says Wittgenstein) are shrugged off or laughed away. They are blotted out by years of schooling and conditioning instead of being encouraged, and so the artist-within is all but killed.

The mystic-within is just as vulnerable, as easily stunted, when at age five or six, the eternal, primeval religious questions first arise: "Who is God, Daddy?" "Who am I?" "Why did my kitten die? Where did it go?"—and are quickly obliterated by evasions or by the ready-made answers of "religious" indoctrination.

To the extent that conditioning and indoctrination fail, the artist-within may still blossom and the mystic-within find scope to ripen—that is, to find his treasure house within. Religious experience is the finding of the treasure house within.

Religious experience is always firsthand experience, utterly personal and subjective. And yet, whosoever has known it recognizes it as being identical with that of others, however different the expressions these others use to describe it, colored by individual, cultural, and linguistic thought-habits and conventions.

There could be no sharper contrast in language than that between Angelus Silesius and a T'ang sage, travelers on the same Way, who would both understand St. Augustine's "You would not have sought me if you had not already found me," as clearly as they would the Zen Master's "If you ask me the right question, your very questioning is the answer!"

"What is the Buddha?" the Emperor asked the sage.

"He is not far from where your question is coming, Your Majesty."

The organized religions, whether Catholic, Protestant or Muslim, have throughout history been frightened by those mavericks who insisted on having their religious experience firsthand and who proclaimed that the "repository of truth" is to be found only in the heart of man.

At best they were shrugged off and pigeonholed as "mystics." At worst they were hanged, burned or quartered according to local preference. . . .

It is as if Angelus Silesius had invented his own Western haiku and doka to express his mystical experience. His verses are hardly longer than those of Ikkyu, thirteenth century:

How marvelous, how god-like the mind of man.

It fills the whole universe! It enters every mote of dust!

Says Ikkyu, and

As Ikkyu does not think of his body

as if it were his body,

he lives in the same place

whether it is town or country.

Angelus Silesius answers with:

How this heart, no larger than my hand,

can enfold heaven, hell, and this wide earth—

This is the mystery no man will ever understand

and:

Unless you find paradise

at your own center,

there is not the smallest chance

that you may enter.

ALBERT SCHWEITZER wrote:

"Mysticism is found wherever a human being sees the separation between the natural and the supernatural, between the temporal and the eternal as overcome and, although still being in the temporal and in the mundane, experiences himself as already belonging to the eternal and the supermundane."

Zen would retort that the natural IS supernatural, that time IS eternity, that the mundane IS supermundane.

THOMAS AQUINAS said:

"Since God is the universal cause of all beings, in whatever region Being can be found, there must be the divine presence."

The Zen Master might answer by being silent, while scratching his left ear with his right hand.

MEISTER ECKHART:

"God is nearer to me than I am to myself. It is just like wood and stone, but they do not know it."

The Zen man would immediately share a cup of tea with him.

JAKOB BOEHME:

"Paradise is still in the world, but man is not in paradise unless he is born again. Then he tastes here and now the eternal life for which he was made."

The Zen Master would never allow him to finish, but cover the "inspired shoemaker's" mouth before he had reached the first comma.

From a Zen point of view the Christian mystics have been handicapped by their concept of God as an objectified Supreme Being. Even when "in union with God" the Christian mystic must automatically exclude that which is not-God. The dualistic split between being/non-being, life and death, oneness-manyness remains. For Zen, the endpoint of man's journey is not "union with God." Zen insists there has never been a separation. All that is needed is the flash of insight that makes one SEE it.

In some of the verses of Angelus Silesius, the Western dualism is still obvious, in others it is completely overcome, as in those in which he speaks of God as Nothingness, as Abyss, and where he reminds one very much of the Mahayana sages, when they speak of Sunyata, the Void, Emptiness. In Buddhist language this Emptiness is also called by more positive words: Suchness, Buddha-Nature.

There is no easy way to explain this Ultimate Mystery. Indeed it cannot be "explained" at all; it has to be experienced. Just to avoid the crudest misconceptions, it has been said that Sunyata is Absolute Emptiness: it does not stand opposed to a fullness.

It embraces the empty as it does the full, for it encompasses all existence and non-existence. One might imagine it as the infinite reservoir from which all arises and into which all is reabsorbed – without ever having been "outside", separated from it. Angelus Silesius seems to have experienced it when he speaks of it as "Seeing Abyss in all that is" and speaks to God as: "Nothingness Thou art." Are Christianity and Mahayana perhaps complementary?

When a Master asked his pupil to show his understanding of Emptiness, the student started to act as if he were catching empty space in his arms.

The Master shook his head: "No good."

"All right, then you show me!" said the student.

The Master grabbed hold of his disciple's nose and gave it a twist. He cried out in pain.

"That is Emptiness taken hold of," said the Master. And at that moment the student experienced Satori, awakening.

Reaching spiritual maturity, enlightenment, is to realize Emptiness, Suchness, as the mystery of our very being, as being our very quintessence. It is the moment that the "Structure of Reality" breaks through, that the Indwelling Spirit overcomes the defenses of the ego, and becomes Self-aware in us.

Some 1400 years ago a brilliant woman, the Empress Wu, ruled over China. She became deeply interested in a new school of Buddhist thought, a totalistic view of the universe, which embodies one of the profoundest insights the human mind has ever attained.

The Hwa Yen sages (Japanese: Kegon; Sanskrit: Avatamsaka) see the Whole, embracing all universes as a single living organism of mutually interdependent and interpenetrating processes of becoming and un-becoming.

The literature in which this cosmic vision is worked out is of extreme complexity, and so the Empress Wu decided to ask one of the Founders of Hwa Yen or Kegon School, Fa Tsang (643 – 712 A.D.) if he could possibly give her a practical and simple demonstration of this cosmic interrelatedness, of the relationship of the One and the Many, of God and his creatures, and of the creatures one to another.

Fa Tsang went to work and appointed one of the palace rooms so that eight large mirrors stood at the eight points of the compass. Then he placed two more mirrors, one on the ceiling and one on the floor. A candle was suspended from the ceiling in the center of the room. When the Empress entered, Fa Tsang lit the candle. The Empress cried: "How marvelous! How beautiful!"

Fa Tsang pointed at the reflection of the flame in each one of the ten mirrors and said: See, Your Majesty: this demonstrates the relationship of the One and the Many, of God to each one of his Creatures. The Empress said: "Yes, indeed, Master! And what is the relationship of each creature to the others?"

Fa Tsang answered: Just watch, Your Majesty, how each mirror not only reflects the one flame in the center. Each mirror also reflects the reflections of the flame in all the other mirrors, until an infinite number of flames fills them all. All these reflections are mutually identical; in a sense they are interchangeable, in another sense each one exists individually. This shows the true relationship of each being to its neighbor, to all that is!...

Of course I must point out, Your Majesty," Fa Tsang went on, "that this is only a rough, approximate, and static parable of the real state of affairs in the universe. For the universe is limitless and in it all is in perpetual, multidimensional motion."

Then the Master covered one of the infinite number of reflections of the flame and showed what we are now, perhaps too late, beginning to realize in ecology - how each apparently insignificant interference affects the whole organism of our world. Kegon expresses this relationship by the formula:

ONE IN ALL

ALL IN ONE

ONE IN ONE

ALL IN ALL

Based on this insight is the Kegon term "The Great Compassionate Heart." This Great Compassionate Heart is not some mythical object. It is the quality of awareness that sees all phenomena (including of course oneself) as part of, as rising out of Emptiness; literally remaining this Emptiness while assuming a temporal form, and finally being reabsorbed by Emptiness.

It is a quality of awareness that quite naturally expresses itself in acts of deepest, yet quite unsentimental reverence and compassion for all that is, the just and the unjust, humans, animals and even plants and stones.

Is the Great Compassionate Heart perhaps what is also called the Holy Spirit?

Then Fa Tsang, in order to conclude his command performance, held up a small crystal ball and said: "Now watch, Your Majesty, how all these large mirrors and all the myriad forms they reflect are mirrored in this little sphere. See, how in the Ultimate Reality the infinitely small contains the infinitely large, and the infinitely large the infinitely small, without obstruction! Oh, if only I could demonstrate to You the unimpeded mutual interpenetration of Time and Eternity, of past, present, and future! But alas this is a dynamic process that must be grasped on a different level...."

The Hwa Yen sutra says: The incalculable aeons are but one

moment, and that moment is no moment, thus one sees the Reality of the Universe....

When I first read this story I was very moved, and I had to construct Fa Tsang's model for myself. I made a version with a candle as center, another with a small Buddha. It is hanging from a tree. Finally I made a version that has the clear crystal ball in the middle, so I may see Emptiness itself, mirroring itself infinitely in all that is. One summer evening as the Hwa Yen model was gently swaying in the breeze, I tried to write down what I had seen in this model of the cosmos:

> There is no peace
> without the Compassionate Heart.
> There is no Compassionate Heart
> without true insight.
> There is no insight
> without the open eye
> that is the seeing
> of that which is not I
> and therefore is I.

of time and eternity

Seen by the eye of faith
the cherry blossoms
are always about to fall.

It is a rare privilege to be born
as a human being, as
we happen to be.
If we do not achieve
enlightenment in this life,
when do we expect to achieve it?
— Echū

Some acts have been considered bad for generations,
and now we do not see anything wrong
with them. It may take centuries to clarify
rules of behavior. Therefore it is foolish
to expect immediate approval.
— Zengetsu

There is that which precedes heaven and earth.
It is formless, nameless.
The eye cannot perceive it. To speak of
it as mind or Buddha is inexact,
then it becomes again something in our
imagination. The Tao cannot be expressed
in words.
— Dai - o - Kokushi

There is no here, no there. Infinity lies before our eyes.
— Sengtsan

A man who has seen into his Self-nature,
sees it whenever questioned about it.
— Hui Neng

Do not compute eternity
as light-year after year.
One step across
that line called Time:
Eternity is here.

The rose that
with my mortal eye I see
flowers in God
through all eternity.

How fleeting is this world...
yet it survives.
It is ourselves that fade from it
and our ephemeral lives.

Were I to lose myself in Him
I'd find again the Ground
that held and nurtured me
before this earthly round.

Eternity is time,
Time, eternity.
To see the two as opposites
is mind's perversity.

Man has two eyes.
One only sees what moves in fleeting time,
the other
what is eternal and divine.

I have known wealth and fame
poverty and utter shame.
Yet all was transitory.
Beyond time I found bliss and glory.

The man in harmony with God
is with himself at ease.
He is content to be here, now
in perfect peace.

Timelessness
is so much part of you, of me -
We cannot hope to find
the self
until aware of our eternity.

Time is of your own making,
its clock ticks in your head.
The moment you stop thought
time too stops dead.

Just one step out of time
I enter God's eternity,
and I am wholly freed
from human transiency.

Until you lose your Me
you cannot see God's face—
The moment you recover it
you fall from grace.

How short our span!
If you once realized how brief,
you would refrain
from causing any beast or man
the smallest grief, the slightest pain.

I am God's alter ego.
He is my counterpart.
In timelessness we merge—
in time we seem apart.

Most sacred:
The Void's immobility
that makes all move,
retaining its tranquility.

At the end of that
which we call history
God is who IS:
for Him there is no past
nor future yet to be.

of the one and the many

A Master was asked:
— What is the Buddha?
— Mind is the Buddha, he answered.
When he was asked the same question again, he said:
— No Buddha, no mind.
Then why did you say before, "Mind is the Buddha"?
— To stop the baby crying! Once the baby stops
crying, I say:
"No mind, no Buddha."

Compassion is the Wisdom,
Wisdom is the Compassion.
— Lankavatara Sutra

The Tao can be shared,
it cannot be divided.
— Chuang Tzu

The meaning of life is to SEE.
— Hui-Neng

In the deep mystery of things as they really
are in themselves, we are released from our
fixations and attachments to them.

— Sengtsan

The Supreme Wisdom (Prajna) is the Oneness
of things; the Supreme Compassion (Karuna) is
the Manyness of things.

— D.T. Suzuki

In the world of Reality there is no self,
there is no other than Self.

— Sengtsan

I know the joy of a fish in the river
through my own joy
walking along the river.

— Chuang Tzu

The mind, the Buddha and living beings,
these are not three different things.

— Avatamsaka Sutra

When the Ten Thousand Things are seen in their
Oneness, we return to the Origin where we have
always been.

— Sengtsan

When Master Nansen was asked:
— Is there any teaching you have not taught
anyone? his answer was:
— Yes. It is neither mind nor Buddha nor
anything.

Every object is the object of compassion...
because no object is an object.

— Anon.

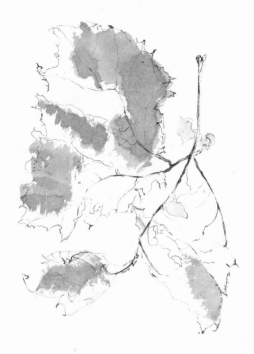

All beings ARE
the Buddha-Nature.
— Dogen

It is not that things are illusory,
but their separateness in the
fabric of Reality is illusory.
— Anon.

The wise have one wish left:
to know the Whole, the Absolute.
The foolish lose themselves in fragments
and ignore the root.

To reflect God in all that is
both now and here,
my heart must be a mirror
empty,
bright,
and clear.

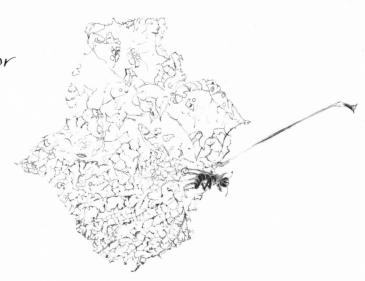

Do not malign
a single thing
for God
not only is its maker
but also its design.

Who is God? No one can tell
He is not dark of night
nor light of day
He is not One nor Many
nor a Father as some say.
Nor is he wisdom,
intellect, or even mercy;
He is not Being—
nor non-Being
neither thing
nor no-thing.
Perhaps He is
what I and all
who ever did or will have being
could ever be capable of seeing
before becoming what He is.

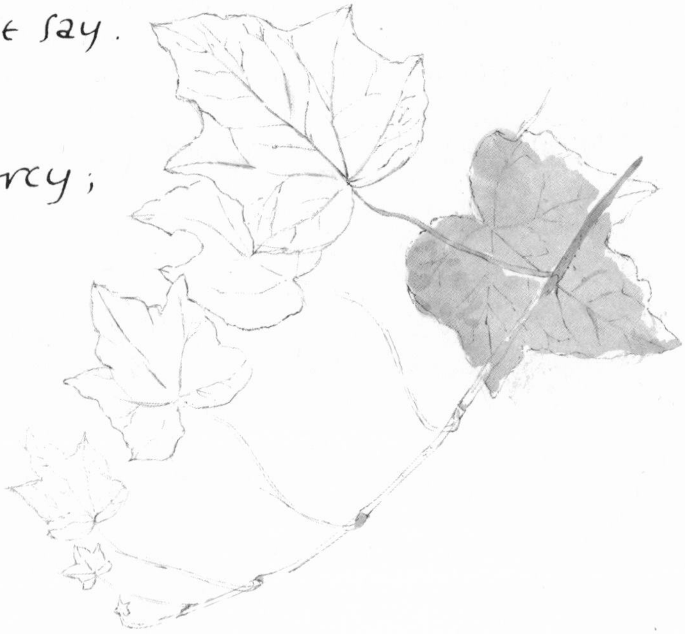

God is the circle's center
for those who dare embrace Him.
For those who merely stand in awe
He is the circle's rim.

A ruby
is not lovelier
than a rock,
an angel
not more glorious
than a frog.

In God all things are one,
He does not separate;
with me as with a gnat
does He communicate.

God is the groundless Ground
with neither size nor limit.
He who is aware of this
has the awakened Spirit.

A raindrop becomes ocean
when it falls into the sea.
Thus does the soul become divine
on seeing its divinity.

He is enlightened,
liberated,
who sees all things as One —
unseparated.

If all God's creatures
do indeed in His undying Word exist,
how can they ever die?
How can they vanish like the mist?

It is as if God played a game
immersed in contemplation;
and from this game
all worlds arose
in endless variation.

No school on earth
can do more than define
that which the Spirit teaches—
to live the life divine.

Until One-ness
has absorbed all Otherness
no man can find
his Suchness.

Love's power
to restore the broken shards
into one whole
is the supreme attainment
of the human soul.

When challenged to explain
the Absolute
I shall fall still,
I shall be silent as a mute.

of ego and the makings of destiny

The emperor came to visit Joshu, who was
meditating in his room.

_Tell him to come in and make his bows, the
Master said to his horrified attendant.

The emperor entered and made his obeisance.
When Joshu was later asked about his rude behavior,
he explained :

_ You just don't understand. If a visitor of low class
comes, I go to the temple gate to greet him. For a
middleclass guest I get up from my seat.
A great emperor cannot be treated like that!

The emperor, of course, had been delighted with his
reception.

God is not nice, God is no uncle.
God is an earthquake!

—Hassidic saying

We are like those who,
immersed in water,
stretch out their hands,
begging for a drink.
— Seppo

We have one moon,
clear and unclouded,
Yet we are lost
In the darkness of the world.
—Ikkyu

58

. He who knows does not speak. He who speaks does not know.

— Lao Tze

Because of our accepting and rejecting,
the Suchness of things escapes us.
The Way is not difficult,
provided we stop picking and choosing.

— Sengtsan

It would be better to consider the body as
ego than the mind. The body at any rate lasts
for a year,
or two years or a hundred, but what we call mind,
thought, knowledge, appears and disappears without trace.
It is in perpetual change.

— Samyutta Nikata

A professor who wanted to know all about Zen
visited a master, who poured tea for his guest, but
kept pouring until the visitor cried:
— Stop, stop! It is running over!
— Indeed, said the master, like yourself! As long
as you are brimming over with opinions and
theories, there is no way to show Zen to you!

There once was a one-legged dragon called Hui.
— How on earth do you manage all those legs,
   he asked a centipede, I can hardly manage one!
— Matter of fact, said the centipede, I do not
   manage my legs.
                                    — Chuang Tzu

A monk asserted:
   — The brilliancy of the Buddha lightens the whole universe.
   — That is a quotation, right?
   — Yes, Master.
   — Well, you are on the wrong track..... A fish who is all
      too greedy is already lost when he sees the hook and
      opens his mouth.

                  He who has attained the Real Mind
                  expresses that Reality whether speaking
                  or remaining silent.

If you want to do a certain thing,
you first have to be a certain person.
Once you have become that certain person,
you will not care anymore about
doing that certain thing.
                                    — Dogen

By honors, medals, titles
no true man is elated.
To realize that which we are,
this is the honor
for which we are created.

All evils —
murder, war and cruel oppression —
from what else do they spring
than from the Me's obsession?

However well of Christ
you talk and preach,
unless He lives within,
He is beyond your reach.

The laws are for the wicked.
Without a single law
the just will love all beings —
holding God's Law in awe.

Believing that you are so smart
and understand it all
Condemns you to ignore
your ignorance—
this is the meaning of the Fall.

Be sure as long as
worldly fancies you pursue
you are a hollow man—
a pauper lives in you.

God does not care
what good you did
but why you did it.
He does not grade the fruit
but probes the core
and tests the root.

The nightingale
does not resent
the cuckoo's song.
But you, if I don't sing"
like you,
mock me as wrong.

Go out and God comes in;
die and in God withdraw_
not_being you will be,
not_doing you will
live His Law.

While gazing at the Sun
I almost lost my sight.
The fault lies in my eye—
not in the Light.

Christ was born a man for me,
for me He died —
Unless I become God
through Him,
His birth is mocked,
His death denied.

Man, the great glutton,
devours the whole cosmos
like a beast.
Then, hungry still,
claims yet another cosmos
for his feast.

A wealthy man obsessed
with profits, deals and losses,
is a poor wretch.
Possessing nothing
he is in truth a man possessed.

In the sun's bright light
We do not go astray
but in the dark of night
how easily we lose the Way.

Oh, foolish Christians
who think you can attain redemption
while with your bodies and your souls
remain attached to worldly goals!

Pity the fool
who thrusts his hand into a flame.
Not . less piteous
the one who fools himself with fame.

She blooms because she blooms,
the rose...
Does not ask why,
nor does she preen herself
to catch my eye.

of life and death

Ah! Summer grasses!
All that remains of the warrior's dreams.
— Bashō

A sick man asked Sengai to write something for the
continued prosperity of his family, to be treasured
from generation to generation. The Master wrote:
— Father dies, son dies, grandson dies.
The sick, rich man was indignant:
— Is that what you write for the happiness of
my family? A tasteless joke, sir!
— No joke intended, said Sengai — If your son
would die before you, that would be very sad. If
your grandson would die before you and your son,
you would be broken-hearted. If your family dies
in the order I have written down, isn't that prosperity
and happiness?
— Sengai

"This existing, that arising", an ancient Buddhist
saying, is not to be understood as meaning
that "this" is the father of "that," as if by a transmission
of substance. This is only the circumstance which
renders possible the arising of THAT.
— Alexandra David-Neel

At a funeral, a monk knocked on the coffin and asked:

— Is he dead or alive?

— I won't say alive, I won't say dead, the Master
replied. This brought the monk to realization.

Whence is my life?
Whither does it go?
I sit alone in my hut
and meditate quietly.
With all my thinking I know nowhere,
nor do I come to any whither:
Such is my present.
Eternally changing — all in Emptiness.
In this Emptiness the ego rests for a while
with its yeas and nays.
I know not where to place them.
I follow my Karma as it moves
with perfect contentment.
                                        — Ryokwan

To what shall I compare this life of ours? Even
before I can say: it is like a lightning flash or
a dewdrop, it is no more.
                                        — Sengai

If you long to transcend life and death,

coming and going, if you want to attain liberation,

you must recognize the man who

is now listening to the Dharma. You who sit here

listening to me, are not

the elements that make up your bodies.

You are that which makes use of these elements.

Be able to see into this truth and you will be

free, whether coming or going.

— Rinzai

I shall not die,
I shall not go anywhere,
I'll be here...
Just don't ask me anything.
— Ikkyu

Of an early death
showing no signs
the cicada sang.
— Basho

All you achieve
must perish
when this world ends.
Therefore become that which you are
and which the world transcends.

Christ is forever
rising from the grave—
the Spirit cannot be
held captive in a cave.

Since God will be my end
let Him be my beginning,
so that I may now fully live
instead of falling, straying, sinning.

In God all that is, is God.
In Him the smallest creature
of the earth and sea
is worth no atom less
than you or me.

Love is like death —
it kills the self-willed Me,
it breaks its stranglehold
and sets the spirit free.

The heart is mighty:
Without breaking His own Law
God cannot flee the human heart,
forsake it and withdraw.

He has not lived in vain
who learns to be unruffled
by loss, by gain,
by joy, by pain.

The sage does not fear death.
Too often has he died
to ego and its vanities,
to all that keeps man tied.

Death does not frighten me,
it only makes me see
how in the here-and-now
life conquers death in me.

You are not real, Death,
for I die every minute
and am reborn in the next
into life infinite.

This body is my enemy and friend.
It ties me down,
is disobedient...
I hate it and I love it_
and when at last we part,
I shall be much relieved,
but... it will break my heart.

The arrow always fails the mark —
will never enter —
If it is I who take the aim
instead of That which is my center.

The heart that grasps
the point
of each contingency
sees the chaos that surrounds it
as pure transparency.

77

If you hope to give birth
to God on earth,
remember: God is not external.
Conception takes place in the heart,
the Womb of the Eternal.

The everlasting Logos
is born anew each day.
Where?
Wherever someone
has cast his Me away.

If Christ were born
within my heart,
He would no longer
have to roam the earth
an outcast, alien by birth.

of heaven and hell

_ Do hell and heaven really exist? a samurai asked.

Hakuin growled:

_ Who are you?

_ I am a samurai.

_ You a samurai? You look like a bum to me! What lord would accept you as a warrior?

Infuriated, the samurai grabbed for his sword.

_ So you do have a sword, huh? It is probably too dull to cut off my head.

As the sword came out of its sheath, Hakuin cried:

_ Here open the gates of hell!

The samurai, impressed with Hakuin's calm, put his sword back and bowed.

—Here open the gates of paradise, said Hakuin.

If anyone by form seeks me,
by voice seeks me,
he walks the wrong path.
          —Vajracchedika Sutra

They do not realize that the ultimate source of sin lies in the three poisons in their mind: greed, anger and delusion. — Hui Neng

Press your eyeballs, and lo and behold: two moons!

— Sengai

Emperor Wu asked Bodhidharma:

— I have built many temples, numberless monasteries.
I had copies made of the sacred sutras, converted
monks and nuns.
What merit have I accumulated?
— None whatsoever, Sire! said Bodhidharma.

It is spring,
In this hut
there is nothing
there is everything.

— Ryoto

When the eternal truth is revealed, this Earth
itself is the Pure Land, this body itself is the body
of the Buddha.

— Hakuin

Ryokan lived in utter poverty in his little mountain
hut. One night a burglar came. He found nothing.
Ryokan surprised the burglar and said:

— You must have come so far to visit me, I
can't let you leave empty-handed.

He took off his clothes and gave them to the
thief, who left nonplussed.
Ryokan sat naked on the floor, watching the moon.

— Poor fellow, he mused — I wish I could
give him this wonderful moon.

81

That which acts in all and meddles in none, is
Heaven (Tao).

— Chuang Tzu

All sins committed
in the three worlds
will fade and disappear
together with myself.
— Ikkyu

It is mind-made : It is like a man painting
a devil, a creature from hell, or a dragon, or a tiger.
He paints it, works on it and gets scared.
All is the brushwork of your own imagination, your
own discrimination!
From the first not a thing is there, except what you
have made out of your own illusive mind.

— Tun-Huang Documents

No thought for the hereafter
have the wise,
for on this very earth
they live in paradise.

All heaven's glory is within
and so is hell's fierce burning.
You must yourself decide
in which direction
you are turning.

Unless you find paradise
at your own center,
there is not
the smallest chance
that you may enter.

Saints do not die.
It is their lot
to die while on this earth
to all that God is not.

The vengeful God
of wrath and punishment
is a mere fairytale.
It simply is the Me
that makes me fail.

No ray of Light can shine
if severed from its source.
Without my inner Light
I lose my course.

Don't think that some tomorrow
you'll see God's Light.
You see it now
or err in darkest night.

We cannot see
the workings of God's hand —
the world has blurred
our eye
as would a grain of sand.

No wonder you despise
the mob's insanity.
All that it demonstrates
is inhumanity.

A man who's steadfast
in joy as in calamity
is one who has
achieved at last
God-given sanity.

What is it not to sin?
I did not ever know
until, one day,
my eye did really see
a flower grow.

Anger is hell's fire.
The moment it is lit,
we fall from our imagined height
into the flaming pit.

God stands far above
the anger, rage and indignation
ascribed to Him
by primitive imagination.

Their eating of forbidden fruit
is not my alibi.
If Eve and Adam had not sinned,
who would have sinned but I?

He whose treasure house is God,
his earth is paradise.
Why then call those
who make this earth a hell
the worldly wise?

You are just dreaming
if you see
the Kingdom
delivered without obligation,
absolutely free.

What is the meaning of Eternal?
It is timelessness.
Time without end
is that which makes
a hell infernal.

of prayer and meditation

_What is the Buddha? a monk asked.

_ Will you believe me? Can I tell you?

_ Of course, Master!

_ Well, you are it!

_ How can I remain it?

_ Ah, if your eye is just the slightest bit
blurred, all you see are hallucinations.

We pray for our life tomorrow.
Ephemeral as life may be,
this is the habit of our mind
that passed away yesterday.
— Ikkyu

The basic idea of asceticism,
leading a life according to the Dharma,
is: to be fundamentally sane.
— Chögyam Trungpa

The mind remaining
just as it was born —
without any prayer
it becomes the Buddha.
— Ikkyu

For fifty years I was a fellow in a straw
raincoat and an umbrella hat. I feel grief
and shame now in this purple robe.
— Ikkyu, when appointed abbot of Daitokuji

90

A monk asks:

— Is there anything more miraculous than the
wonders of nature?

The master answers:

— Yes, your awareness of the wonders of nature.

Your treasure house is within.
It contains all you will ever need.
Use it fully instead of
seeking vainly outside yourself.
— Hui Hai

When looked at in the light of Tao
nothing is best, nothing worst.
Each thing is in its own light,
stands out as it is.
— Chuang Tzu

The Zen experience is like a sense experience: it is
direct, it needs neither symbolism, nor constructs of
thought.

— D.T. Suzuki

Zen practiced in the state of activity
is incomparably superior
to that practiced in the state of withdrawal.

                    — Daie

The Truth, Reality, is grasped by the mind,
not by sitting in meditation.

                    — Hui Neng

If you seek the Buddha outside of the mind,
the Buddha changes into a devil.

                    — Dogen

How often have I prayed
"Lord do your will"...
But see: He does no willing —
motionless He is and still.

The deepest prayer
which I could ever say
is that which makes me One
with That to which I pray.

God is such as He is,
I am as I must be.
And yet no two-ness
do I see.

There is nothing
that disturbs your meditation
but your own wandering mind
in its vain agitation.

The moment that you pause
to rest upon the Way,
you fall behind,
you are pulled back,
you go astray.

God hears above
all hollow noise
the echo of His praise
in every creature's voice.

Give me all your bounty,
give me eternal bliss —
as long as You withhold yourself
all things I miss.

Be still and empty:
He shall fill
you with far greater fullness
than you could ever
wish or will.

So far beyond all words
is He,
I know no other way
than not to speak.
Thus without words
I pray.

In the depth of His Abyss
God is pure Contemplation.
The deepest ground
of all that is
dwells in perpetual adoration.

What do the blessed do?
Concerned no more
with "yours" and "mine"
they stand in the Eternal Presence,
the Divine.

We keep so busy talking,
we are so keen to act
that we forget
that in the heart
lies all we need
untapped, intact.

How out of tune
your pious whine
with the awesome harmony
of the divine . . .

He who turns the senses
to the Light that is his center
hears what no ear can hear,
sees where no light can enter.

Prayer is neither word nor gesture,
chant nor sound.
It is to be in still communication
with our Ground.

of the inner light and enlightenment

A Zen monk asked his friend to help him solve the riddle of life. The friend said that he would do as much as he could, but that there were a few things everyone has to do for himself.

— For instance?

— Well, if you are hungry or thirsty I can't eat and drink for you, so that is up to you. Then, I can't go to the bathroom for you, so that you will have to take care of. And, third, you'll have to carry your own body along the road.

This gave the monk, the insight he searched for.

All the teachings the sages expounded in the Buddhist, the Taoist, and the Confucian classics are no more than commentaries on your sudden cry:

— Ah, this!

— Daie

A man went into a butchershop. The butcher was cutting up a pig.

— Please, cut me a really fine slice of meat.

The butcher threw down his knife, and said:

— Sir, can't you see this is all really fine meat?

The man had a sudden realization.

— What is the Buddha, Master?

— You have no Buddha Nature!

— Then what about the animals?

— They do have the Buddha Nature!

— And why should I be devoid of it?

— Because you have to ask
  and do not recognize it yourself.

The perfect man uses his mind as a mirror.
It grasps nothing, it rejects nothing.
It receives but does not keep.
— Chuang Tzu

In what I have shown you, there is nothing secret
or hidden. If you reflect within yourself and
recognize your own face which was before the
world, the secret is within yourself.

—Hui Neng

When an individual monad is perceived as reflecting
eternity, there is satori. I lift a finger and it covers the
whole universe.

— D. T. Suzuki

Things are SUCH AS THEY ARE. For who does not
understand this, things are JUST AS THEY ARE.
Nevertheless, things remain SUCH AS THEY ARE.

— Gensha

Walking is Zen, sitting is Zen;
whether we speak or are silent,
move or are still,
it is unperturbed.

— Yungchia

Sentient beings are
intrinsically Buddhas.
It is like water and ice:
apart from water no ice can exist.

— Hakuin

— What happens when an enlightened man slides
back into delusion? a monk asked.
— A broken mirror does not reflect properly,
fallen flowers do not jump back onto the branch!

Do not search for Truth. Just stop having opinions.

— Sengtsan

The clearer I perceive
that which is True,
the less reasoning, judging, arguing
I can do.

The deeper my insight
into the Real,
the less I talk
of what I see and feel.

Now that my eye
has seen the essence of the mind,
no words that could describe it
can I find.

The longest way to God,
the indirect,
lies through the intellect.
The shortest way lies through the heart.
Here is my journey's end
and here its start.

Unknowable, unnamable,
You seem the other pole.
And yet
my human heart
contains You Whole.

God is abundance,
His gifts beyond all measure.
My heart is bewildered —
afraid to hold such treasure.

As great as God I am,
as small as I is He.
How could I below Him
or He above me be?

Desire returns
as soon as we ignore
the divine essence
at our core.

The Clear Light
cannot be attained
until both heart and mind
have deepest Insight gained.

a State of attention

Christ could be born
a thousand times in Galilee —
but all in vain
until He is born in me.

Do not seek God
in outer space —
your heart is the only place
in which to meet Him
face to face.

With hope and trust
we sow the seed

in the dry earth —
Thus is the Kingdom sown,
trusting and hoping
for its birth.

Mysterious Being
infinitely far from me,
who yet
in every beating
of this heart
must be.

A heart awakened has eyes:
perceives
the Light
in dark of night.

A man awakened
is all joy —
though all is lost,
he lost merely a toy.

I am not outside God.
He is not outside me.
I am His radiance;
my light is He.

God is the constant love
that breathes
in all life I see.
Oh that His wisdom
and compassion
lived in me!

No sweeter tone
from any lute could spring
than when
this heart and that of God
resound
as with one string.

All proofs and arguments
cannot distort the sight
of him who is awakened
to his own Inner Light.

of God and the true self

— What was Bodhidharma's reason for coming
to China?
— Why are you so concerned with Bodhidharma
instead of with yourself?

— I came here to find the Truth, Master.
— Why wander around? Why do you neglect your
precious treasure at home?
— What do you call my precious treasure?
— That which asks the question is the treasure.

— All these mountains, rivers,
this whole great earth,
where does it all come from?
— Where does your question
come from?
— Cheng-tao Ke

— What is the deepest meaning of Buddhism,
Master?
The Master made a deep bow to his pupil.

Hui Neng asked a monk who came to see him:

— What is it that thus walks toward me?

After pondering the question for eight years, the monk found the answer:

— Even to say it is something does not hit the mark.

Another monk answered this question:

— It is no "what."

— Is there any special way to discipline oneself in the Tao?

The master nodded.

— What is it, Master?

— When hungry one eats. When tired one sleeps.

— Isn't that what everybody does?

— Not at all!

— Then what is the difference?

— When they eat, they don't just eat, they indulge in worries and imaginings. When they sleep they are given to idle dreams. That is their way, but their way is not my way.

                              — Hui Hai

One day Hyakujo said to his monks:

— Plow this field and when you are all finished,

  I'll tell you the meaning of everything.

When they had finished, he gave his sermon:

He opened his arms wide. Then he left.

Master Zuigan talked to himself every day :

— Good morning, Master !

— Yes, I am here.

— Wake up, wake up !

— Yes, yes, I have !

— In future don't be fooled

  by others !

— No, I won't, I won't !

    —Mumon

Wherever I may be, I meet him —
He is no other than myself,
Yet I am not he.   —Dosan

It is not on the Master that the "secret" depends,
but on the hearer. The Master can at most open the door.
    — Alexandra David-Neel

114

A philosopher came to the Buddha and asked:

— Without words, without the wordless, will you
tell me the Truth?

The Buddha remained silent.

The questioner thanked him profoundly, saying:

— By your loving kindness I have cleared all
delusions and entered the Path.

After he had gone, Ananda asked the Buddha to
explain what had happened. The Buddha said:

— A good horse runs even at the shadow of the whip.

— Buddhist Scripture

All the Buddhas and Bodhisattvas are
his servants. Who is he?
Whoever sees him clearly, feels as if he has
met his own father on the street corner—
he does not have to ask others
if he is right or wrong.   — Mumonkan

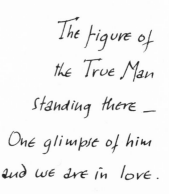

An ordinary human being is a Buddha. Illusion is
salvation. One foolish thought and we are stupid,
ordinary. The next awakened thought and we are
the Awakened One, the Buddha.

— Hui Neng

The figure of
the True Man
standing there —
One glimpse of him
and we are in love.

— Ikkyu

How do we perceive our Self-Nature?
That which perceives is our Self-Nature. Without
it, there could not be perception.

A blind man visited his friends. It was dark when
he left, and they gave him a lantern.
— Thank you, but I don't need it. Light or
dark, it is all the same to me.
— Yes, but carry it anyway, so people won't bump
into you.
Off he went, and soon someone collided with
him and shouted:
— Why don't you look where you're going!
— Why don't you see my lantern?
— Sorry, brother, said the other — your candle
went out.

Gautama and Amida too
were originally human beings.
Have I not also the face of a man?
          — IKKYU

Within our impure mind
the pure one is to be found.
        — Hui Neng

— Who are the Buddha's parents?
— His father's name is Smith; his mother's
name is Pretty face.

The creatures are
the Word's
perpetual incantation,
in rapture as in dread
sounds its reverberation.

It is meaningless to say
"Thy will be done,"
and yet to pray
"Please take this agony away."

There is no higher aim
than to reclaim
another, blinded by life's pain—
to make him live and see again.

I am as rich as God.
Each dust mote
more or less
do I in common
with my God possess.

I am a tower
raised in God
and from my utmost height
Survey His measureless domain
in awe and in delight.

If you could just be still,
stop rushing round and round
in search of God —
You'd find Him as your Ground.

See what no eye can see,
go where no foot can go
choose that which is no choice —
then you may hear
what makes no sound —
God's voice.

Am I then like the sun?
Must I color with my rays
the untinged ocean
of God's ways.

My heart could receive God
if only it chose
to turn toward the Light
as does the rose.

Do not cry out to God.
Your own heart is the source
from which He flows unceasingly
unless you stop its course.

God is a phantom
drifting by —
until you see Him all around you
and stop asking
who?   what?   why?

The saint forgets
all about God's commands.
He acts spontaneously
as love of man — and God — demands.

You wander far afield,
think you must roam the earth
instead of diving deep into yourself
to find your real worth.

I do not face my end in fear
for, knowing death must come,
I let my Me die long ago
and watched desire disappear.

No death has greatness
but that from which new life
can spring,
No life more vital
than that which from the death
of Self takes wing.

# of bondage and freedom

Chien Nin used to carry the rice box to the dining hall himself, while dancing and calling out:

_ Come and eat, you Bodhisattvas!

Then he roared with laughter and clapped his hands.

_ What do you think the Master means by carrying on like this? a monk asked.

_ It looks as if he is singing praises, said his friend.

They asked another Master:

_ Whom does he praise?

By way of answer this teacher got up and danced.

The monks bowed in thanks.

_ What do these bows mean? the Master asked.

One of the monks started to dance.

The Buddha raised a flower before the gathering of his disciples and none could fathom the meaning of this act except Mahakasyapa, who smiled softly and nodded. Thereupon the Buddha transmitted the Eye of the Dharma to Mahakasyapa, his successor.

When asked about his training system, Hui Neng said:

_ If I should tell you that I have a system of law to transmit, I would be cheating you. All I do to my disciples is to free them from their own bondage, by any means their case may need.

Whether you are bound by a gold chain or an
iron one,
you are in captivity. Your virtuous activities are
the gold chain, your evil ones the iron one.
He who shakes off both the chains of good and evil
that imprison him, him I call a Brahmin —
he has attained the Supreme Truth.

— Buddhist Scripture

A Master asked his disciple:

— Why don't you read Scripture?
— What is the difference between Scripture and
  Zen?
— Well, even if you don't need it for yourself,
  do it for the other people's sake.
— The patient himself has to overcome the illness.

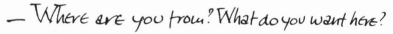

— Where are you from? What do you want here?
— I am from the South, Master, and I want to
  attain awakening.
— Those barbarians from the South have no Buddha-
  Nature! How can you expect awakening?
— There may be Northerners and Southerners, Master,
  but as to the Buddha-Nature that makes not the
  slightest difference.

One of his disciples asked the Buddha:

— If I should be questioned about my Master's opinion, what shall I say?

— You shall say: The Venerable One holds no opinions. He is freed of all opinions.

        — Buddhist Scripture

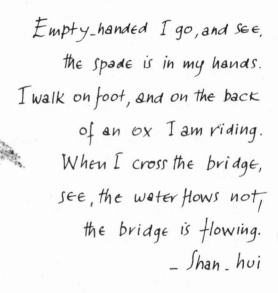

Empty-handed I go, and see,
  the spade is in my hands.
I walk on foot, and on the back
  of an ox I am riding.
When I cross the bridge,
  see, the water flows not,
  the bridge is flowing.
    — Shan-hui

The Original Mind (BUDDHA-NATURE, BODHI, SELF-NATURE, TRUE SELF, COSMIC UNCONSCIOUS, ORIGINAL FACE, SUCHNESS, SUNYATA, ESSENCE OF MIND) is to be recognized along with the working of the senses and thought. Yet it is neither dependent on nor independent of the senses and thought.

        — Huang Po

When one no longer believes in the "I",
when one has rejected
all beliefs, the time has come
to bestow gifts.
—Buddhist Scripture

A monk asked:

— Please help me: Show me how to attain liberation.

— Who has bound you? the Master questioned him.

— No one has bound me.

— Then why ask me to be released?

The monk had a profound realization.

When a disciple beseeched Joshu to give him
instruction, the Master said:

— Have you had your breakfast?

— Yes, Master.

— Then go and wash your bowls!

The monk was enlightened.

Obeying our self-Nature we are in accord with
the Way and wander freely without annoyances.
— Seng tsan

Nothing keeps you bound
except your Me —
until you break
its chains, its handcuffs,
and are free.

Although a thousand steel bars
shackle me,
Yet I shall be unbound
for I am free.

He who is detached
from pain and freed from quest
acts by his very being,
travels while at rest.

To see the light at all
I must first leap across
all barriers,
destroy the Me's defenses,
tear down its wall.

He who boasts that he is free
from craving, owning, knowing,
only proves his strivings and illusions
are still growing.

Let go of the Me
as of a worthless thing —
Unless you abdicate
you will not be a King.

When pleasures cease to please
and grief no longer causes pain
you may be closer to release
than you believe.

The emptier I do become,
the more delivered from the Me,
the better shall I understand
God's liberty.

I was God inside God
before I became Me
and shall be God again
when from my Me set free.

You who did create
and can unmake this earth,
You cannot force
against my will
my second birth.

The True Self of all that is,
is quintessential —
remains itself, unchanged,
outlasting all that's incidental.

It is our will that
gets us lost or found.
It frees me now,
as once it kept me bound.

He who hopes to make true art
must remember from the start
that nothing true can be created
unless by Spirit permeated.

Who freedom loves
loves God
and only he is free
Who freed from all desire
in God finds liberty.

of the central mystery

Form is the Void, and the Void is Form.
The Form is nothing else but Form,
and the Form is nothing else but the Void.
Outside the Void there is no Form,
and outside the Form there is no Void.
— Nagarjuna

The infinitely small is as large as the
infinitely big. Limits are nonexistent.
The infinitely large is as small
as the infinitely minute.
No eye can see their boundaries.
— Sengtsan

Outside the Buddha
there is no mind,
outside the mind
there is no Buddha.
— Baso

And the Ocean God said:
Can one talk about the ocean
to a frog in a well?
Can one talk about the Tao
to a learned philosopher?

— I come to you with nothing,
  said the monk.
— All right, just drop it!
  Joshu answered.
— But I just said that I have nothing,
  What is there to be dropped?
— Then just carry it away with you!

The Emperor asked Bodhidharma:
— What is the basic principle of the sacred Doctrine?
— Vast Emptiness, Sire, and nothing in it to
  be called sacred.
— Who is it who is now confronting me?
— I know not, Sire.

The Master asked a novice:

— Where did you come from?

— From Suzan, Master.

— What is it that thus comes?

— One could not say it is similar to any thing.

The Self-Nature, unmoved in itself, is able to produce all things.
— Hui Neng

If you break open the cherry tree where are the blossoms? But in Spring time how they bloom!

— Ikkyu

It cannot properly be called the Void or not-Void or both or neither. Just in order to point at it, it is called the Void.
— Madyamika Scripture

"Everything is," is one extreme.
"Nothing is," is the other.
Between these two I teach the truth of Interdependent Origination.
— The Buddha

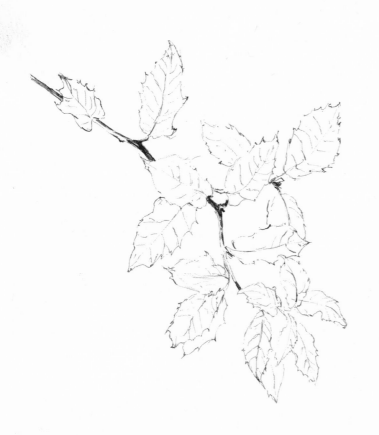

How this heart
no larger than my hand
can enfold heaven, hell,
and this wide earth
this is the Mystery
no man will ever
understand.

All the unfolding, growth,
and Evolution we are seeing,
all this changing and becoming...
God sees as timeless Being.

I know, but don't know why,
that without me
God cannot live
nor without Him
can I.

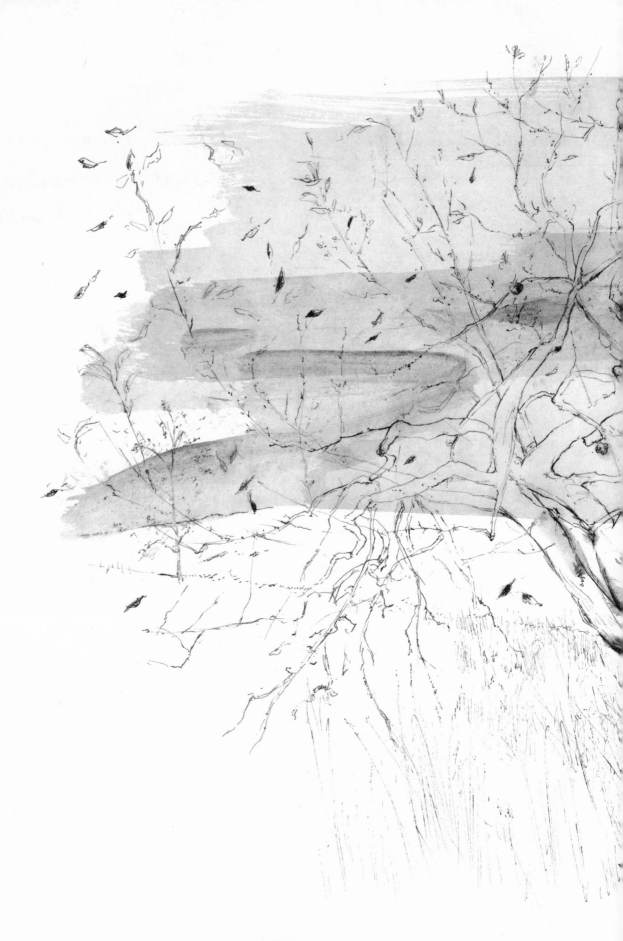

If you dare
call Him "Father"
and live this in reality
You must become
a newborn child
and overcome duality.

God is sheer Nothingness.
Whatever else He be,
He gave it
that it might be found
in me.

Deepest well
from which all rises, grows.
Boundless ocean
back into which
all flows.

When I am neither
you nor me,
when there is no more here
nor there —
then I begin to be
of God as Nothingness
aware.

Eternal Spirit, who manifests
all that the eye perceives,
formless, nameless Mystery
which no mere human mind
conceives.

Nothingness You are,
fathomless Abyss.
To see Abyss in all,
is seeing
that which Is.

142

You are all that enters mind
and yet remain
such as you are.
Eternal Spirit
by form
nor name confined.

Who sees the All as Nothingness,
as Nothing all that is,
sees as if through God's own eye—
Enlightenment is his.

He is pure Nothingness.
He is not now, not here.
I reach for Him
and see Him disappear.

You are the fire,
I the reflected glow.
How could I without You,
You without me grow?

Is there still hope
I may be growing
toward the Wisdom
that is not-knowing?

I know not who I am,
but what I know, I'm not—
a thing, yet a no-thing,
a circle, yet a dot.

God, the Formless
creates Himself as Form,
becoming
structure and substance,
lightness, darkness,
stillness, storm.

De profundis,
my heart cries out
to the divine Abyss.
Which of the two
the deeper is?

Now I must end,
Beloved.
If you would read more,
look deep into your heart:
all Scriptures'
root and core.

FREDERICK FRANCK, whose drawings and paintings are part of the permanent collections of a score of museums in America and abroad, including the Museum of Modern Art, the Whitney Museum, the Fogg Museum and the Tokyo National Museum, is an uncommonly versatile man. He holds degrees in Medicine, Dentistry, and Fine Arts. For three years he served on the staff of Dr. Albert Schweitzer at Lambaréné. He was the only artist to record all four sessions of the Second Vatican Council (1962-1965).

His many books deal with Africa and Albert Schweitzer, with religious experience, and with his concept of drawing. In his best known book "The Zen of Seeing", he speaks of drawing as a spiritual discipline, an equivalent of meditation and prayer.

In memory of Pope John XXIII, for whom he has unbounded admiration, he converted the ruins of an eighteenth-century watermill near his house in Warwick N.Y., into "PACEM in TERRIS", a "trans-religious oasis of inwardness." Among the artistic and spiritual events at "Pacem in Terris" are workshops on "seeing/drawing as meditation", and performances of. Franck's own contemporary version of the medieval Play of Everyman.

A NOTE ON THE DESIGN AND PRODUCTION OF THIS BOOK:

The book was printed and bound by The Murray Printing Company, Forge Village, Massachusetts.

The hardbound version of the book was bound in Kennett, a natural finish cloth supplied by Joanna Western Mills Company, and Multicolor paper supplied by Lindenmeyr Paper Corporation.

Display Calligraphy by Janet Papazian

The book was designed by Susan Mitchell.